ASSUME NOTHING: A MANUAL FOR BUYERS OF AMERICAN AND ENGLISH ANTIQUE FURNITURE

ROBERT F. WEINHAGEN, Jr.

Illustrated by Mary Dowling

Robert F. Weinhagen, Jr. was born and raised in White Bear Lake, Minnesota. He was educated at the University of Minnesota and Harvard Law School. Since the early 1970s, he has studied and collected 18th century American and European furniture. He is an Associate Counsel, the Office of Legislative Counsel, U.S. House of Representatives.

Mary F. Dowling is a free–lance artist from the Pacific Northwest. A native of Centralia, Washington, she currently resides in nearby Tenino, where she specializes in commercial art for individual and corporate clients.

"One does not require an expert, but an actuary, to tell the collector of English furniture that, in one year, more is shipped to America than could have been made in the whole of the eighteenth century."

-- Herbert Cescinsky
The Gentle Art of Faking Furniture (1931)

For my dear wife, Laura.

CONTENTS

PREFACE

Perhaps beginner's luck does exist. One day in the fall of 1972 I was walking along a sidewalk in Kensington, Maryland. I happened to be on a stretch that the locals called "antiques row." I had never given a thought to antiques. A set of eight mahogany dining chairs with needlepoint seats was displayed in the window of a barber shop. An antiques dealer had rented the space. I really liked the set of dining chairs, but of course had no idea what I was looking at. I bought them anyway.

I decided to learn what I could about the chairs. I purchased a book entitled *American Antique Furniture: A Book for Amateurs*, an old classic by Edgar Miller of Maryland. The chairs were scroll-back chairs with saber legs that dated to about 1820-1830. Illustration No. 317 in Edgar Miller's book depicted an identical chair.

I then began visiting North Howard Street, the "antiques row" of Baltimore. In my meanderings I entered the antiques shop of Harry Berry, Jr. I bought a small 18th Century Chippendale fret mirror and asked him about my set of eight chairs. Later I brought him one of the chairs and he stated that it was part of a larger set that he knew had descended in some Maryland families. Hence footnote #3 next to chair Number 64 (another chair in that same set) in the book entitled *Furniture in Maryland, 1740-1940*, published by the Maryland Historical Society.

I was learning the lesson of the importance of knowledge. It is invaluable to read about antiques and to get to know antique shop proprietors.

Next, I learned the importance of perseverance. But I was also reminded of the old saying "Strike while the iron is hot!" In the mid-1970s a local Alexandria, Virginia, dealer was offering a period George II (ca. 1750) mahogany camelback sofa. While I contemplated the sofa, someone else bought it. I quickly learned that an affordable, period 18th century sofa is exceedingly difficult to find. Five or six years later I decided to call back the dealer. He remembered the sofa because it was the only period Chippendale sofa he ever had in his shop. He said the buyer had moved to the Maryland eastern shore. He gave me the man's name but did not know his address. I tried long-distance information for various eastern shore towns until I located him. He was willing to sell the sofa. I bought it over the phone, borrowed a truck, and picked it up that weekend. After loading the sofa in the truck, I asked, "Why are you willing to sell me that sofa?" He replied, "Because a neighbor of mine who was a big man would come and visit and he would invariably plop himself down in the center of the sofa. I was sure he would break it, but I just couldn't say anything to him. It was easier to sell the sofa to you."

Many prized antiques transcend the ownership of any individual. They have an indefinable value of their own because of their importance to the individual collectors who have been entrusted with their ownership and care. In the mid-1970s I met a retired clock dealer, Nel, who graduated from Barnard College in 1929, lost her job on Wall Street when the stock market crashed, and then moved with a friend to southern Maryland to work on a tobacco farm. The two women bought a small farm in Oakton, Virginia, during the Great Depression and started farming. Nel learned to repair antique clocks and her friend to repair and refinish furniture. Their antiques business flourished on the farm until the 1960s when they retired. Over the years Nel and I became close friends and when she died she willed me her favorite tall case clock that she had steadfastly refused to sell to anyone. Why?

She believed the clock was hers to keep but not to sell. In the 1940s an older clock collector became a good customer of hers. Unfortunately his brother was crazy and painted all the clocks he collected. One special tall case clock made in the 1790s by John Way of Waggon Town, Pennsylvania, had been given to him by another collector. His brother promptly painted it black. When her friend was quite old he gave it to Nel, someone who would appreciate it. Nel restored the clock to its original condition. This John Way tall case clock is one of my most prized possessions.

Sometimes you have a feeling that certain things are meant to be. In 1980 a good friend, Leonardo, telephoned. His next door neighbor had left a severely damaged late 18th century English oak tall case clock for the trashmen to remove. Leonardo expressed an interest and the neighbor gave him the clock. He asked me to secure a reliable clock repairman. I offered to buy the clock, but he declined. He wanted to give it to his brother in Duluth. The clock was repaired and sent by rail to him. While being unloaded, the crate was dropped. The clock was repaired again in Duluth.

Eight years later I decided on a whim to visit Leonardo. We walked through his garage and there stood that exact tall case clock on the concrete floor next to his car. Imagine my surprise! His brother had retired and returned the clock to him in Alexandria. I asked, "What are you going to do with the clock?" Leonardo replied, "Sell it to you." It is upstairs in my home now.

Beginner's luck, perseverance, timing, trust and friendship, fate, learning, and plain hard work are some of the elements of successful collecting.

CHAPTER 1. GENERAL INTRODUCTION

Purpose

The purpose of this manual is to generate a healthy skepticism that antique furniture offered for sale is genuine and to increase the likelihood that you, a buyer of antique furniture, will have the requisite knowledge to decide if a piece is genuine, extensively repaired, or a fake. It is written from the perspective of a buyer of late 17th, 18th, and early 19th century American and English furniture. Its author is a collector, not a dealer, auctioneer, picker, museum curator, appraiser, or other member of the antiques trade.

Collectors are primarily interested in one aspect of the antiques trade: acquiring attractive, high-quality, genuine antiques for their homes. The discriminating collector wants furniture that was hand-made by craftsmen and is a part of our heritage. He wants something tangible as a legacy for his children and their children or, perhaps, as a contribution he can make to our cultural history.

Unfortunately, a collector's first concern has to be authenticity. There are simply too many fakes in the marketplace today. Some are domestically produced, but many are imported from Europe, as Herbert Cescinsky, one of England's foremost furniture experts, pointed out in 1931. The number of fakes is still burgeoning; that has been a persistent problem throughout the 20th century.

A thorough knowledge of furniture styles and appropriate

1

methods of construction are necessary for the serious collector but are insufficient to enable that collector to distinguish fake from authentic. Why? Because a good faker will construct a piece of furniture by hand using old woodworking techniques and the stylistic features will be correct. Yet the piece is not "of the period."

Historical Perspective: What Goes Around Comes Around

After the Philadelphia centennial exhibition of 1876, there was a revival of interest in 17th and 18th century furniture. This led to price inflation and wholesale production of both machine-made and hand-made colonial revival furniture.

Faking 17th and 18th century furniture became financially rewarding by the beginning of the twentieth century. An article in "Good Housekeeping" (February 1906) stated: "About ninety percent of the things sold nowadays as antiques are bogus." A 1909 United States consular report, entitled "Trade in Alleged Antiques", cited numerous examples of fake English, Dutch, French, and Italian furniture being imported into the United States as legitimate antiques. It was estimated that the majority of such furniture being imported in the first decade of this century from Europe were spurious pieces.

In the 1920s there was another revival of interest in 17th and 18th century antiques and consequent price inflation. It was a new heyday for fakes and reproductions.

Concern about fakes was widespread in the 1920s and 1930s. A famous highboy sold in 1929 for the unheard-of price of

$44,000. In the March 29, 1930, issue of the "Saturday Evening Post," Wallace Nutting, the prominent New England collector and author of *Furniture Treasury* (1928), stated: "They [the buyers] would have been far more startled had they known that the styles of carving on the two parts of the highboy had nothing to do with each other." Mr. Nutting also lamented about fake foreign antiques being passed as legitimate American pieces to fetch more money. In his seminal work, *American Antique Furniture, A Book for Amateurs* (1937), Edgar Miller, the great Maryland collector and author, warned about pervasive faking of antique American and English furniture.

A Federal appraiser at the port of New York quoted in the January 9, 1926, "Saturday Evening Post" said that over two-thirds of pieces imported through New York as antiques were fakes. In the May 15, 1937, issue of "Literary Digest", the U. S. Treasury Department, the agency responsible for tariff law enforcement, estimated that between 75 and 85 percent of "antiques" imported into the United States from 1906 to the mid-1930s were fakes.

If Federal officials and antique furniture experts were concerned about fakes escaping detection in 1906, 1909, 1926, 1928, 1930, and 1937, imagine what their level of concern would be today! How much more difficult do you believe it is to detect those fakes today, over three-quarters of a century later?

In his book, *Is It Genuine?* (1971), W. Crawley, an English cabinetmaker, cites first-hand knowledge of shops where "antique" furniture is being made. He also mentions the practice of "face-lifting" Victorian and Edwardian furniture into more desirable, earlier period pieces.

3

Even new fakes can fool experts. In the late 1970s, Armand LaMontagne, a Rhode Island wood sculptor, made by hand a 17th century style turned arm chair. A chair at Pilgrim Hall in Plymouth, Massachusetts, was the copied object. He gave the fake chair to a friend who was a dealer. Its new life had begun. The fake went through the hands of various dealers and was eventually purchased by the Henry Ford Museum in Dearborn, Michigan, for approximately $9,000.

Robert Bishop, the consulting furniture curator at the Henry Ford Museum, included the chair in his book *How to Know American Antique Furniture* (1973). The museum illustrated the chair on the cover of a brochure.

Briefly, LaMontagne made the fake chair as follows. He felled a tree and turned the wood while it was still green so that it would shrink into an elliptical shape. He constructed the chair using 17th century techniques, but bore an inconspicuous hole with a modern drill bit (to be able to later prove the chair was a fake). He beat, bruised, burned, and bleached the chair. He then put on a thin layer of glue, followed by dust. After that, he waxed and smoked the chair. He then bathed it in salt water and bleach to remove the smoky smell. This finishing process was repeated a few times. Meanwhile the chair was painted various colors. He further damaged it by removing 2 spindles. Finally, he aged the chair in the Atlantic Ocean.

The Henry Ford Museum continued to exhibit the chair for 4 years after being told of the hoax by the New Hampshire dealer who sold it to them. An article in the Detroit Free Press caused the museum to have the chair x-rayed, which proved that a modern

4

drill bit was used. The museum acknowledged the chair to be a modern fake. The price they paid for this rare antique was too good to be true!

A more recent incident further illustrates that no one can be too careful, even a museum. The July 1992 issue of *Maine Antique Digest* reported that the Bennington Museum in Vermont disclosed that a piece included in its recent publication "Highlights from the Bennington Museum" (1989) as a western Massachusetts highboy from 1789 and displayed as authentic for 15 years was a fake. It was assembled in about 1920 from 18th, 19th, and 20th century parts.

If history teaches us anything regarding antique furniture, it is that as antiques become more popular and more costly fakes abound in the marketplace. Nowadays the collecting of antiques is quite fashionable. Decorators comb flea markets and antique shows and shops with abandon. There is a proliferation of shows and flea markets. The old guard has always lived with antiques; the nouveau riche are discovering them.

In closing the historical perspective portion of this chapter, mull over this question: Where are all of these fakes today? Are they being offered for sale at fashionable shows, shops, and auctions? Let's hope they neither are nor will be situated in your homes.

Introduction

A burgeoning demand, an ostensibly fixed but geographically scattered supply, and ever increasing prices of late

17th century to early 19th century American and English furniture; some owners' lack of knowledge of the true worth of their old furniture; many buyers' desire to get something for nothing; and some peoples' natural gullibility and others' natural guile have created an antiques trade rife with shenanigans.

If you visit a shop, the owner will tout his pieces and usually react unfavorably to questioning their authenticity. Remember, he is the seller, not an objective third party.

If you attend an auction, nothing that is said by the auctioneer or stated in the catalogue matters because the written terms of the auction always specifically waive reliance on any oral or written representations. It is difficult not to participate in the chase.

If you are in a private home in response to an advertisement, the item for sale typically belonged to a great grandmother, has a greatly inflated value to the owner, and was in the family as far back as even the grandmother could remember. Expect exaggeration.

If you are in a private home for an estate sale, the atmosphere will be chaotic because people generally wait in line for hours at the crack of dawn to be one of the first to gain entry. The pressure to buy is intense. It is hard to examine a piece that may be sold out from under you. The family probably kept the best antiques and the person conducting the sale may add other difficult to sell pieces. In all of these situations, like it or not, as a buyer, you are on your own. How can you help yourself? Read books on furniture style and construction and examine major museum collections and reputable private collections. Study this manual and assemble the tool kit it recommends. Use them when examining antique furniture to enhance your chances of passing at appropriate times and buying for the right reasons.

Whether furniture sold as genuine was made as a fake or an honest colonial revival reproduction is immaterial. You want to buy what you are paying for. Buying antiques may be your avocation, but it is usually the seller's vocation. Assume nothing when buying antique furniture.

CHAPTER 2. EVERYTHING BUT THE REAL THING

Fakes

Most experts agree that a great many fake antiques exist in the marketplace. Fakes may appear in many guises:

(1) Creations from scratch from old wood.

(2) The union ("marriage") of two or more antiques, such as a chest-on-chest or desk and bookcase that were not made together. A variant would be to make a large set of chairs from a smaller number of antique chairs because large sets command more money per chair.

(3) Antiques that contain significant, unacknowledged replacement parts, such as replaced tops, legs, or pedestals. Old wooden floor boards make nice tabletops, sides for tall case pieces, and drawer fronts.

(4) Conversion of an antique into a more desirable piece, such as converting a chest into a kneehole desk, 2 chairs into a settee, or a spinning wheel into a tilt-top table, or reducing a chest to a more salable size.

(5) Antiques remade from parts of other antiques, such as a lowboy made from the base of a highboy or a chest made from the upper part of a highboy.

(6) Antiques "improved" to enhance their value by new carving or inlay, reveneering, or bogus labels.

(7) Legitimate, old reproductions made by craftsmen such as Wallace Nutting and sold initially as reproductions but subsequently as period antiques.

Repaired Pieces

In 1950, Albert Sack, a posh New York City antiques dealer, wrote *Fine Points of Furniture: Early American*, in which he categorized the effect of repairs on the value of antiques. Nowadays many experts view his criteria as too restrictive. Nevertheless, repairs such as a new or spliced leg on a chair, replaced feet on a chest of drawers, or a new top on a table do adversely affect value. A dealer may be less than candid in identifying repairs; an auctioneer will probably say nothing.

The ideal antique is in pristine condition. Unfortunately most of those are found only in museums or exceptional private collections. The few that are for sale command prohibitive prices. Therefore, as a buyer, you will most likely find repaired or restored antiques and will be faced with 3 tasks: (1) discovering any repair or restoration, (2) determining how much it reduces the fair market value of the antique, and (3) deciding whether you still want to buy the antique.

Some repairs are unavoidable. If a leg is missing, it has to be replaced for the antique to be useable. But repairs do adversely affect fair market value.

While it is difficult, and perhaps foolhardy, to endeavor to correlate market value and particular repairs or restorations, nevertheless I have prepared the following general guidelines. At the least, they will serve as a warning to study antiques very carefully before buying them.

A minimal repair such as the following may cause a 10 to 25 percent reduction in an antique's fair market value: replaced molding, drawer lips, backboards, bottom, cornices, aprons, door panels, interior desk drawers, banisters, spindles, mirror glass, or back legs. Slight warping would also cause this reduction in value.

A more extensive repair such as the following may cause a 25 to 50 percent reduction in an antique's fair market value: a replaced slant front desk lid, front leg, arm, exterior drawer, crest rail, splat, reverse painting, or bonnet top; replaced face or works of a tall case clock; reshaped drop leaves or reshaped headboard or footboard on a bed; part of all legs, feet, or stretchers being replaced; or the marriage of 2 antique cases.

An even more extensive restoration such as the following may cause a 50 to 75 percent reduction in an antique's fair market value:

(1) For a chair: all arms, legs, stretchers, or spindles replaced, or recarving or reshaping the splat.

(2) For a sofa: all arms, legs or stretchers replaced, or being reduced in size.

(3) For a table: all legs or the top replaced.

(4) For a chest of drawers, chest-on-chest, or highboy: reduced size, all drawers or a top replaced, or reveneering the entire piece.

(5) For a desk or secretary: reduced size, a new upper or lower case, or replacing all of its drawers.

(6) For a corner cupboard: replaced doors, or a new upper or lower case.

(7) For a bed: headboard, footboard, or 2 posts replaced, or recarving or returning the posts.

(8) For a tall case clock: a replaced hood or the

case being reduced in size.

The wholesale restructuring of an antique by making it into a different furniture form would reduce its value by at least 80 percent. Making a chest of drawers into a kneehole desk or a tall chest into a highboy are examples.

An antique's value is also affected by the quality of its exterior surface. Original surface on finished or painted furniture is most sought after. An old but not original surface that has some patina will reduce value by about 20 percent. A stripped and sanded or newly repainted surface will reduce value by about 50 percent.

Rarity of Certain Pieces

Be suspicious if a period antique is offered for sale at a price that is too good to be true. Respect the relative scarcity of genuine antique furniture: 17th century furniture is exceedingly rare; 18th century furniture is very rare; and early 19th century furniture is rare.

Within these periods, certain furniture forms are more or less common than others. For instance, butterfly tables are probably the rarest form of American antique furniture; gateleg tables are very rare; tavern tables are rare; and tilt-top tables are much more common. Queen Anne mirrors are extremely rare; Chippendale mirrors are rare; and Empire mirrors are commonplace.

CHAPTER 3. PERIODS AND STYLES

(a) A Classification of Periods:

    (1) Mid to late 17th century.

    (2) William and Mary - 1690-1730.

    (3) Queen Anne - 1730-1760.

    (4) Chippendale - 1750-1800.

    (5) Hepplewhite - 1790-1815.

    (6) Sheraton - 1800-1830.

(b) An Alternate Classification of Periods:

    (1) Pilgrim - 1620-1720.

    (2) Colonial - 1720-1776.

    (3) Federal - 1776 to about 1830.

(c) Additional Considerations Regarding Periods:

    (1) Periods generally extend to later dates in rural areas than in urban centers.

    (2) Periods are a few years later in America than in England.

(d) Styles

    (1) Styles may evolve and diminish within a period.

    (2) Styles of more than one period may be combined

in an antique, especially country furniture. Many antiques are transitional between 2 styles.

(3) An antique must be dated by its latest stylistic feature.

(4) Some forms of furniture were created during a particular period:

(A) Highboys, lowboys, and slant-front desks first appeared during the William and Mary period.

(B) Windsor chairs did not exist before the Queen Anne period.

(C) Chests-on-chests began during the Chippendale period.

(D) Sideboards first appeared in the Hepplewhite period.

(E) Dressing tables with attached mirrors first appeared in about 1800.

(F) Coffee tables did not exist before the 20th century.

CHAPTER 4. NECESSARY TOOLS

Tool Kit for Examination of Furniture

The following tools are necessary for a thorough examination of furniture: low-power magnifying glass, 10x small lens, flashlight, calipers, straight edge, tape measure, pocket knife, magnet, screwdriver, and pliers.

How to Use This Manual

First, read it from cover to cover.

Second, form an overall impression of an antique by considering some of the general questions set forth below; if it seems wrong, do not buy it.

Third, if your overall impression is favorable, then examine the antique to determine its genuineness by applying the relevant factors described in chapter 5 to the examination and studying the furniture parts referred to in chapter 6.

Fourth, if you still believe that the antique is desirable, begin an in-depth analysis of the type of furniture (chair, desk, chest, etc.) being examined as set forth in chapter 7.

Doing these steps takes patience and effort; there are no short cuts to discovering the truth.

Overall Impressions and First Encounters

The overall first impression of an antique is very important.

Stand back and study it; form an impression. In what style period was the antique made? Are its proportions and stylistic details correct for that period? Does the piece appear authentic?

Additional questions to consider include the following:

(1) What woods were used to make the antique?

(2) Is it American or English?

(3) Is the method of construction appropriate to the period?

(4) Is there a consistency of construction methods throughout the antique, especially if it has 2 parts?

(5) Is there evidence of the use of modern tools?

(6) Is its wood of random thickness and hand-cut?

(7) Is there authentic wear?

(8) Is there proper shrinkage?

(9) Has it been refinished?

(10) Have there been extensive repairs?

(11) Has it been improved or made over?

(12) Is the antique of too small a size or scale for the 17th or 18th century? Was it cut down?

Next, start the actual examination of the antique. Look at its back and top, remove the drawers (if any), turn the antique upside-down, and look inside and underneath using the tools recommended above and the knowledge acquired below.

CHAPTER 5. GENERAL FACTORS TO CONSIDER IN THE EXAMINATION OF ANTIQUE FURNITURE

Shrinkage

All wood shrinks across its grain. In certain situations, shrinkage can be measured with a tape measure or calipers. Expect evidence of shrinkage on genuine antiques. But shrinkage alone will not prove that an antique is 17th or 18th century because even a 100-year-old antique will exhibit shrinkage.

What You Should Expect Regarding Shrinkage:

(a) A round or square tabletop will no longer be perfectly round or square. A round top on a table with a 3 foot diameter would shrink about one-half inch across its grain (figure 1).

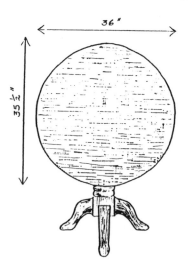

1. *Crossgrain shrinkage*

2. *Caliper measuring crossgrain shrinkage*

(b) Turned parts of furniture, such as table or chair legs or ball feet, will be slightly oval (fig. 2).

(c) Wide furniture boards that are attached to an underframe, such as one board forming the side of a chest, will have split or cracked (usually at its midpoint because this is the weakest point).

(d) Boards that originally abutted each other, such as tabletops, sides of chests, bottoms of drawers, or backboards, will have gaps between them.

(e) Tabletops and leaves will shrink and perhaps warp: tops of 17th century gate-leg tables may have warped and leaves of Pembroke tables may have "spread-eagled" because they have become smaller than the frames to which they are attached.

(f) Breadboard ends of a tabletop or lid on a slant-front desk will be slightly longer than the width of the abutting board.

(g) The case door of an antique grandfather clock will have

narrowed and this may be discernable.

(h) Square Chippendale legs will no longer be perfectly square.

(i) Veneer may crack or buckle because of shrinkage of the wood beneath the veneer, such as a veneered grandfather clock case.

(j) Applied molding along the edge of a board will tend to separate from it.

What You Should Not Expect Regarding Shrinkage:

(a) Round tabletops to be perfectly round.
(b) Turned legs or pedestals to be perfectly round.

Wear

Antique furniture is old. Assume it was used for its intended purpose, and analyze its wear or lack thereof in terms of that use. Expect wear to make sense.

What You Should Expect Regarding Wear:

(a) A front stretcher of a chair will have deeper wear on its upper side and closer to the legs than at its midpoint, and if a chair has 2 front stretchers, the lower one should be more worn (fig. 3). Side stretchers will show some wear, but back stretchers should be almost pristine.

(b) Backs of finials of tall chairs such as banister-back or

3. *Stretcher wear*

other turned chairs should be flattened with wear (fig. 4).

(c) Outsides of front and back legs and feet of chairs and tables will be bruised, dented, and perhaps rounded or partially worn away.

(d) Bottoms of feet of chairs, tables, and stools should look

4. *Chair finial wear*

polished and smooth with fine lines, have closed grain, and be cracked or gouged.

(e) A drawer bottom will show wear in the form of a concave line, unless repaired (fig. 5).

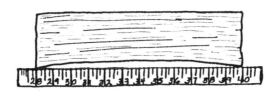

5. *Drawer bottom wear*

(f) Chair arms and handholds should show considerable wear.

(g) Molding along the top edge of a table should no longer have sharp edges or corners.

What You Should Not Expect Regarding Wear:

(a) No wear at all.

(b) Illogical wear, such as even wear on all of a chair's stretchers or numerous distress marks over the entire surface of an antique.

(c) Not finding wear where you would expect it, such as the outside edge of a front chair stretcher, bead molding along the edge of a drawer, or molding along the edge of a tabletop.

Color of Unfinished (Secondary) Wood Surfaces

Different kinds of wood age differently. Therefore, the comparisons referred to in this manual will always be of different pieces of the same kind of wood.

Exposure to air, light, moisture, and dirt causes unfinished wood to darken over time. Two factors affect this darkening process: the location of the unfinished wood on a piece of furniture and the duration of time since it was newly cut. Expect the color of unfinished wood to be uniform; it should vary in its degree of darkness in a predictable manner solely because of the above factors. Newer wood (such as a later replacement) or protected wood (such as a small drawer inside the well of a slant-front desk) will appear brighter and lighter than older, more exposed wood.

Many antique furniture experts consider this aging of unfinished wood surfaces and the resulting gradations in color (usually shades of brown) to be the single most important indicator of an antique's authenticity.

What You Should Expect Regarding Unfinished Surfaces:

(a) All wood that is in a similar location on an antique should show the same change in coloration:

(1) The outside of all backboards should be a uniform color, almost black.

(2) The inside of all backboards should be a uniform color, but much lighter than their exposed side.

(3) The inside of a case piece should be a uniform color where boards meet, such as a side board meeting a backboard or the underside of the top, or a backboard meeting the underside of the top.

(4) The top edge of a drawer side should be the same color as the side it meets.

(b) Wood in different locations on a piece should show different degrees of color change:

(1) The bottom of a chest will be darker than the back.

(2) The underside of the lower chest of a chest-on-chest will be darker than the underside of the upper chest.

(3) The underside of a drawer will be lighter than the back or bottom of the chest, and the underside of a small drawer inside the well of a desk will be lighter still.

(4) New unfinished wood or a new saw cut on old wood is quite light; the contrast between it and the surrounding wood would be so great that a faker would have to stain or finish it to disguise his handiwork.

(c) Different kinds of unfinished wood age differently:

(1) Tulip poplar becomes gray.

(2) White pine becomes reddish brown.

(3) Most other woods will darken to shades of brown.

What You Should Not Expect Regarding Unfinished Surfaces:

(a) The inside or underside of a case piece to be finished,

stained, or painted, which would have been done to hide newer wood or work.

(b) Backboards of case pieces or exposed edges of secondary boards to be finished, stained, or painted.

(c) Any part of a drawer (other than the exposed front) to be finished, stained, or painted.

(d) The underside of a tabletop to be finished, stained, or painted.

(e) Adjacent surfaces of unfinished wood of non-uniform color.

(f) Exposed top or bottom edges of backboards to be too light or bright, indicating a modern replacement or an old board being cut down.

(g) Unfinished surfaces that appear smoky or muddy, which may indicate that they were stained.

Patina of Finished (Primary) Wood Surfaces

Patina is a difficult concept to describe. Patina is a soft, smoky look which finished wood attains by centuries of exposure to air, dirt, and wax. These old, finished surfaces appear to have depth; they are almost translucent.

What You Should Expect Regarding Patina:

(a) Patina on finished surfaces, unless an otherwise genuine antique has been recently refinished. The surface should look mellow and appear to have slight undulations.

(b) Tops of tables should be smooth and the wood grain closed because they have been scrubbed and waxed for centuries. For example, if the grain of oak is wide with black speckles, the oak is too new to be 17th or 18th century.

What You Should Not Expect Regarding Patina:

(a) A finished surface with a flat, plastic-like appearance, unless recently refinished.

(b) Wood grain that appears quite open, which is a characteristic of newer cut wood.

Painted Surfaces

An antique with original paint is much more valuable than a repainted or stripped piece. The paint history of an antique is useful to ascertain its age and discover any replaced boards. Scraping paint with a knife shows the number of layers of paint and whether the bottom layers are brittle.

What You Should Expect Regarding Paint:

(a) A muted color because old paint deteriorates by exposure to sunlight, heat, and moisture.

(b) The paint to be brittle and hard and consequently to chip or powder when scrapped with a knife.

(c) Not being able to dent the paint with your fingernail.

(d) No paint smell.

(e) Some alligatoring or cracking as it shrinks.

(f) Paint to be worn away where the antique had the most use.

(g) All surfaces to exhibit the same paint history:

(1) To examine a case piece for paint history, remove the drawers and look inside the front corner of each drawer opening and the edges where the front and sides of each drawer meet.

(2) To examine a chair, look at an area just covered by upholstery or where the leg and seat frame meet.

(3) To examine a table, look at the underside of the top near each leg.

(h) Black, red, and yellow colors were prevalent from the 17th century and blue became popular in the early 19th century.

(i) Gray and other colored milk paints were first used in the 1830s.

(j) An antique's painted surfaces should feel the same; if a surface feels different than the other surfaces, then it may indicate a replacement.

What You Should Not Expect Regarding Paint:

(a) A bright paint color.

(b) The paint to come off in ribbons (curls) when scraped with a knife.

(c) The smell of paint.

(d) Being able to dent the paint with your fingernail.

(e) Uniform, pristine paint surfaces throughout.

(f) Drip marks, which may indicate new work.

(g) Paint in cracks or gaps where boards have separated or worn areas (such as table or chair stretchers), which would indicate that the piece was painted after the cracks, separation, or wear.

(h) A board without traces of paint found on other boards, which may indicate a replacement.

(i) Paint that fluoresces bright purple under a black light, which happens with new paint.

Wood Size; Saw and Other Tool Marks

Boards used in the 17th and 18th centuries were wider and thicker than boards used on modern furniture. Unfinished boards should have hand tool and saw marks as described below.

What You Should Expect Regarding Wood Size and Marks:

(a) Boards used to make furniture in the 17th and 18th centuries were at least 20 inches wide; and the sides of case pieces and tabletops and leaves were usually made from 1 board.

(b) High quality wood; knots were unusual on primary surfaces.

(c) Boards, such as tabletops, at least 1 inch thick.

(d) Back boards of case pieces of random widths.

(e) Hand-plane marks on the undersides of drawer bottoms or on back boards of furniture will feel like slight, parallel ridges and hollows because cabinetmakers used jack planes with convex blades (fig. 6). Use a straight edge and light or move your fingers

6. *Hand-plane marks*

gently across the surface to discern these marks. Hand-plane marks are not usually found on furniture made after 1850.

(f) Look for straight, parallel lines at least one-quarter inch apart and usually perpendicular to the wood grain (marks from the manual pit saw will be slightly angled) on unfinished surfaces of boards that were hand or mill sawn (fig. 7). These saw marks would date the wood before 1840.

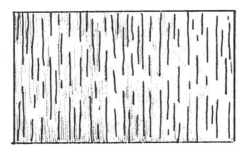

7. *Mill saw marks*

What You Should Not Expect Regarding Wood Size and Marks:

27

(a) Boards of modern thickness, such as 7/8 or 16/25 of an inch.

(b) Circular saw marks (distinctive, parallel marks that curve), which date the board to 1840 or later (fig. 8). Examine drawer bottoms and lower edges of backboards.

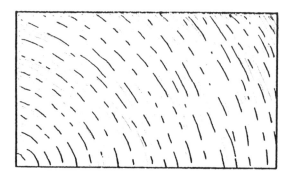

8. *Circular saw marks*

Nails

Hand-forged nails were used in the 17th and 18th centuries. Machine-cut nails were first made in the early 19th century. The modern gimlet nail was first made in 1880.

Examine all nails. Nails found in 17th or 18th century furniture should be hand-forged; nails found in early 19th century furniture should be machine-cut or hand-forged. You should not find round, pointed, gimlet nails, except for a later repair.

Examine all nail holes. Round nail holes were made by modern gimlet nails and do not pre-date 1880. Rectangular holes were made by machine-cut nails and do not pre-date 1800. Square holes could have been made in the 17th or 18th century.

What You Should Expect Regarding Nails:

(a) Exposed wood adjacent to a nail head should appear blackened and rusted; there should be no gap between it and the nail head.

(b) Hand-forged nails in 17th and 18th century furniture should exhibit the following characteristics (fig. 9):

(1) Square shank.

(2) Show marks of a forger's hammer.

(3) Taper on 4 sides to a point.

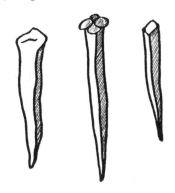

9. Early hand-forged nails

(4) Square, T or L shaped, or "rose" (bumpy) heads, or be headless.

(5) No 2 nails are the same.

(6) Rust resistant because they were made from very pure iron.

(c) Hand-forged nails were used in the 17th century on blanket chests, Bible boxes, and early drawers.

(d) Machine-cut nails in 19th century furniture (usually

made before 1850) should exhibit the following characteristics (fig. 10):

(1) Two parallel and 2 converging sides which end in a blunt point.

(2) Thicker and less tapered than handmade nails.

(3) No hammer marks.

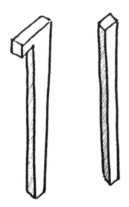

10. Machine-cut nails

(4) Superficial, parallel ridges or burrs perpendicular to the nail's edges, which were made by a cutting machine.

(5) Tendency to rust.

(6) Usually have L shaped heads, not rose heads.

What You Should Not Expect Regarding Nails:

(a) Raw wood or gaps around nail heads, which would indicate the nails were recently applied.

(b) Nails that are countersunk and puttied over.

(c) Modern machine-made steel wire nails, except for a modern repair (fig. 11).

(d) Rose-head nails with blunt ends and the same bumps on their heads, because they are reproductions.

(e) Round holes (which would have been made by modern wire nails), except for a modern repair.

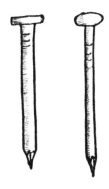

11. *Modern wire nail*

(f) Rectangular holes on furniture made before 1800, unless the result of a later repair.

(g) A rusty nail head and no darkened adjacent wood, which would indicate the nail was not original and probably recently applied.

(h) Upon removal, a totally rusty nail, which would indicate a reused old nail.

Screws

Early handmade screws appeared in America in about 1720 and

were used instead of nails to secure hinges and locks and to hold tabletops to frames, cleats to lids, and chest of drawer tops to frames. Small brass knobs on drawers inside slant front desks were screwed in. Corner blocks were sometimes screwed into place. But the widespread use of screws occurred after the Revolution.

Machine-made screws with blunt ends were widely used from about 1800 to 1850. Modern gimlet screws with pointed ends appeared after 1850.

What You Should Expect Regarding Screws:

(a) Early handmade screws on late 17th and 18th century furniture should exhibit the following characteristics (fig. 12):

(1) Rounded, uneven threads.

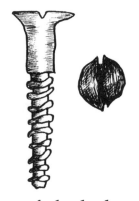

12. *Early handmade screw*

(2) Heads are out of round and flat and sometimes have visible file marks.

(3) The slot for the screwdriver is irregular, off-center, and has little depth.

(4) Tips usually come to a dull point.

(5) Shorter than one-half inch long.

(6) Shank is never exactly round and it tapers.

(b) Early machine-cut screws on 19th century furniture (before 1850) should exhibit the following characteristics (compared to early handmade screws) (fig. 13):

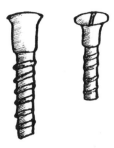

13. *Early machine-cut screw*

(1) Ends are blunt.

(2) Threads are more uniform and tend to be sharper.

(3) Heads are almost round.

(4) May be longer than one-half inch.

(5) Shank has no taper.

What You Should Not Expect Regarding Screws:

(a) Modern gimlet-point screws with sharp, even threads that taper to a point on furniture made before 1850, unless the result of a modern repair (fig. 14).

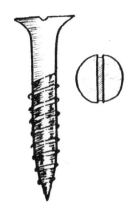

14. *Modern gimlet screw*

(b) Any screws in 17th century American furniture or early machine-cut screws in 17th or 18th century furniture, unless the result of a modern repair.

Hardware

Hardware refers to hinges, knobs, brasses, and locks. Rarely will a 17th or 18th century antique have its original hardware intact. Nevertheless, empty or plugged holes provide valuable evidence of the history of hardware used on an antique. This history is a useful clue to an antique's authenticity.

What You Should Expect Regarding Hinges:

(a) Expect hand-forged hinges on furniture made before 1820 or evidence of their earlier presence.

(b) On 17th and early 18th century cupboard doors and lids of blanket chests, dower chests, and Bible boxes, expect either_

(1) cotter-pin (staple) hinges, which are 2 hand-wrought, thin iron rods up to 1/8th inch thick, bent over, linked together, and clinched into the wood (fig. 15); or

(2) later hinges, but upon examination, evidence of earlier cotter-pin hinges: hinge marks & 2 small holes in the wood the pins passed through.

15. *Cotter-pin hinge*

(c) Before 1750, on table leaves or cupboard doors, expect either:

(1) butterfly hinges, which, when opened, resemble the wings of a butterfly (fig. 16), and -

16. *Butterfly hinge*

(A) which were made by bending 2 pieces of hand-forged iron over an iron pin and hammering them together; therefore, look for hammer marks;

(B) each leaf of which is tapered toward its edges, rough, and irregular;

(C) were attached with hand-forged screws or rosehead nails, clinched back or riveted over small iron washers; and

(D) the holes of which were handpunched (so there should be a lip on one side) and never truly round; or

(2) later hinges, but upon examination, evidence of earlier butterfly hinges.

(d) During the 18th century, hand-forged, iron strap hinges attached with hand-forged screws or rivets, especially on sea chests, dower chests, and large blanket chests, but not table leaves (fig. 17).

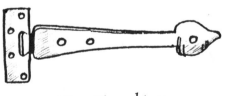

17. *Strap hinge*

(e) During the 18th and early 19th centuries, hand-forged H, HL, & rattail shaped iron hinges attached with hand-forged nails or screws to the outside of cupboard doors (fig. 18).

(f) From the 17th century to about 1820, rectangular iron butt hinges were used primarily on drop-leaf tables (fig. 19). Each half of this hinge is 2 thicknesses because each half was bent and welded together. A pin unites the 2 halves. The hole into which the pin is inserted is not perfectly round. These hinges were usu-

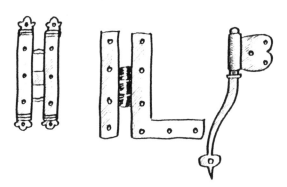

18. H, HL and rattail hinges

-ally mortised into the wood. If the hinge is gone, expect to find the mortise or a wood patch in its place.

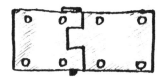

19. Butt hinge

(g) From about 1820 to 1850, cast iron hinges (which may have been replaced by machine-made bent-steel hinges), which were usually mortised into the wood and commonly used on tables and insides of cupboard doors.

(h) Always expect early hand-forged hinges or evidence of such on furniture made before 1820. If an antique has cast-iron hinges and no marks of older hinges, then it postdates 1820.

(i) If hinges on pre-1820 furniture are not hand forged, then expect either:

(1) an outline (because of dirt and wax buildup) on the wood where earlier butterfly, strap, H, HL, or rattail hinges were attached, or

(2) a shallow mortise or evidence, such as wood fill, of a former mortise into which earlier butt hinges were set.

What You Should Not Expect Regarding Hinges:

Cast-iron or modern hinges on furniture made before 1820 and no marks of older hinges.

What You Should Expect Regarding Wooden Knobs:

(a) Before 1730, a wooden knob was longer than wide; rarely more than 1 inch in diameter or more than 2 inches long; and attached either by being nailed from behind, by a wooden pin through a hole in its shank, or by the back of the knob that was a dowel pounded through a small hole into the drawer front (fig. 20).

(b) After 1730 and before 1840, wooden knobs were wider than long (like mushrooms) and attached as above or from behind by screws.

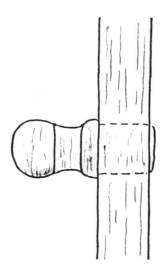

20. Early wooden knob

(c) An exception to the general rule expressed above is some 19th century Shaker furniture. The Shakers revived the use of the very early wooden knobs.

What You Should Not Expect Regarding Wooden Knobs:

Wooden knobs that were attached from behind with modern machine-cut screws, which would have been the case after 1850.

What You Should Expect Regarding the History of Brasses on an Antique:

Rarely are original brasses found on an antique. Any holes or plugged holes that are not being used by the present brasses are evidence of the history of brasses that were used.

First, expect holes in locations appropriate for the period

of the antique. For instance, a 17th century drawer should show evidence of former William and Mary drop pulls and backplates: one centered hole with cotter-pin marks on the inside of the drawer front, wear on the front of the drawer where the drop pull hit the wood, and patination where the plate protected the wood.

Second, expect old holes that are not perfectly round.

Third, on a 2-part case piece expect a history of brasses that is identical on all drawers of both parts. The number of holes and the distances between them should be the same on each drawer of identical size as should the shadows of earlier brasses; otherwise, the cases may be married.

What You Should Expect Regarding Brasses:

(a) If a brass is original to an antique, expect the following:

(1) Undisturbed encrustation surrounding the brass resulting from wax and dirt build-up.

(2) If you remove the brass, the wood underneath should be fresh and have a nice patina.

(3) No evidence of earlier brasses: no plugged holes and no faint outline present of a different shaped escutcheon.

(4) The brass to have a mellow patina and be pale yellow in color.

(5) You should feel slight surface variations on the brass.

(6) If there is any chasing, it should vary from plate to plate.

(7) The mounts should not be identical and should have marks of the finishing file on their edges because of hand trimming and finishing.

(8) The backside of the brass should be pitted because it was sand cast.

(9) All escutcheons on an antique should be in a line and centered on each drawer (from top to bottom).

(10) The bottom of a pre-1840 key-hole opening should be round (fig. 21).

21. *Early keyhole escutcheon*

(b) In the case of teardrop pulls (from about 1670 to 1730) (fig. 22):

(1) The plate is usually thin, flat, and plain, but may have a pierced or stamped (but not engraved) geometric design.

(2) The drop may have a flat or hollow back; the whole pear was not cast until the late 18th century.

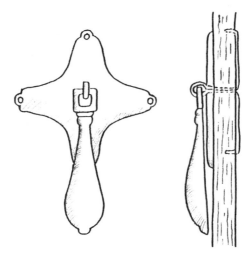

22. Teardrop pull

(3) Secured to the drawer by one cotter pin, the only traces of which may be a single hole (that may be filled with a wood plug), an outline of the plate, and 2 clinch marks on the inside of the drawer front.

(4) Expect to find marks on the drawer front caused by the drop constantly banging against it.

(c) In the case of cotter-pin bail handles (from about 1700 to 1740) (fig. 23):

(1) Stamped with punches (not engraved) and with chamfered edges.

(2) Attached to the handle by 2 cotter pins.

(3) The bails attached to the posts from the inside.

(d) In the case of bat wing mounts (from about 1730 to 1800) (fig. 24):

(1) A cast knob was part of the plate into which the

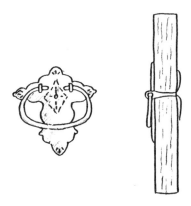

23. *Cotter-pin bail handle*

ends of the loop handle were engaged on the inner sides of the knobs.

(2) The posts were cast square and secured the plate to the drawer by the use of cast metal nuts.

(3) Cast metal nuts had crude threads and were thin, odd-sized, and made of brass.

(4) Small round-headed brass pins held the plates and keyhole escutcheons to the drawers.

(e) In the case of willow mounts (from about 1750 to 1800) (fig. 25):

(1) Used on Chippendale furniture.

(2) Originally 2 to 3 inches between postholes, the distance of which generally grew in the later part of the period.

(3) The bail handles attached to the posts from the inside.

(f) In the case of bail handles held with bolts on rosette

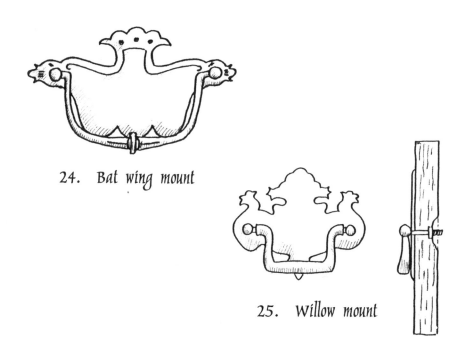

24. Bat wing mount

25. Willow mount

mounts (from about 1730 to the early 19th century) (fig. 26a):

26a. Bail handle on cast rosette mounts

    (1) The shank of the bolt was normally cast in a square cross section.

    (2) The threads were coarse, rough, irregular, and very shallow because they were cut by hand.

(3) Before 1790 rosette mounts were cast and exhibited surfaces scraped by hand with slight irregularities along their edges; after 1790 they were stamped from sheets (fig. 26b). Reproductions were usually made from thin sheets of brass.

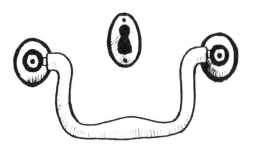

26b. Bail handle on stamped rosette mounts

(4) The bails attached to the posts from the inside.

(g) In the case of oval mounts (from about 1790 to 1820) (fig. 27):

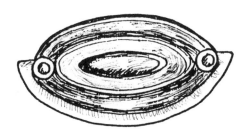

27. Oval mount

(1) Used on Hepplewhite pieces.

(2) The plates were die stamped, had delicate

patterns, and were made from thin sheets of brass.

(3) The bails attached to the posts from the outside.

(4) The shank of the bolt was usually cast in a square cross section.

(h) In the case of round (rosette) knobs (from about 1800 to 1840) (fig. 28):

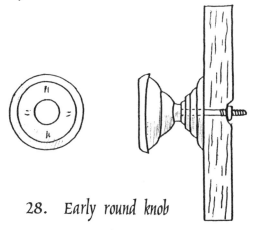

28. *Early round knob*

(1) Used on Hepplewhite and Sheraton pieces.

(2) Usually stamped from sheet brass and filled to add weight.

(3) A screw was permanently soldered in place and a threaded nut secured the knob from the back.

(i) In the case of cast brass hinges (from the mid-18th to the mid-19th century):

(1) English cast-brass butt hinges or H-hinges with iron pins were available from early Colonial times for use on high quality furniture.

(2) Usually attached with hand-made iron screws or both iron screws and brass pins.

(3) Not strong and most have been replaced, especially slant-front desk lid hinges.

(4) Expect slight imperfections in their shape and on their surface and pitted back sides.

(5) Supplanted by sheet brass hinges in the mid-19th century, which were machine-stamped, smooth, and much stronger.

What You Should Not Expect Regarding Brasses:

(a) Posts that are round, threads that are machined, and nuts that are large and exactly square, because these would be characteristics of reproduction brasses (fig. 29).

(b) Ivory escutcheons, except on small objects such as tea

29. *Reproduction round knob*

caddies; they were not used on cabinet pieces until the Victorian era.

(c) A square bottom on a key-hole opening, which is a Victorian practice (fig. 30).

30. Victorian keyhole escutcheon

(d) Handles that are not in the center of a drawer or that appear too large for the drawer, which may indicate the drawer or the piece has been tampered with.

(e) Unusually large brasses, because 18th century cabinet makers favored smaller brasses.

(f) Brasses that were machine stamped and smooth to the touch.

(i) To attract a magnet, because brass is not magnetic.

What You Should Expect Regarding Locks:

(a) Most drawers had locks.

(b) Locks had square or oblong stubby bolts, and high quality locks had 2 or 3 such bolts.

(c) Locks were brass, but levers and bolts were steel.

(d) If there is a lock or a mortise on a drawer indicating that there was a lock, the bottom of the adjacent rail should show evidence of a mortise for the bolt to enter.

(e) Locks were usually screwed into an area chiseled into the back side of the drawer front. Below the lock should be 2 parallel saw cuts that relate to the hole for the lock which is narrower than the covering plate.

(f) Expect replacement locks and evidence of earlier locks if there are replacements.

(g) Locks were attached by clinched nails or handmade screws.

(h) An English or American lock turns counterclockwise and bolts with one turn; a French lock turns clockwise twice to engage its locking pins.

What You Should Not Expect Regarding Locks:

(a) No pre-Victorian lock should be stamped with a name, patent number, or the word "patent". If there are file marks on either side of the levers, it once had a name or patent there.

(b) Bolts with circular shafts, which would indicate the lock is Victorian, unless it was a replacement lock.

(c) Thin locks with broad bolts, which are usually later 19th century locks.

Joints

A joint is formed where 2 pieces of wood meet and are

held together. It is useful to be able to identify the sorts of hand-made joints that were used in furniture construction before the mid-19th century and the sorts that were not.

What You Should Expect Regarding Joints:

(a) Butt and rabbet joints were used in 17th century. But, in the case of country furniture, sometimes until the mid-19th century (fig. 31).

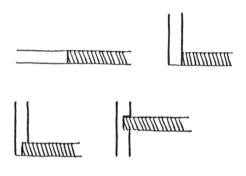

31. *Butt and rabbet joints*

(b) Hand-cut dovetailing started in the very late 17th century (fig. 32a). Early 18th century drawers had 1 or 2 wide (usually from 2 to 4 inches), stubby, crude dovetails. By 1725, 2 or 3 narrower, but still wide, stubby, dovetails (fig. 32b). By about 1775, thin and delicate appearing dovetails (fig. 32c).

(c) Expect mortise (rectangular or round) and tenon joints to be used in the 18th and early 19th centuries (fig. 33).

(d) Until about 1840, the ends of mortise holes and socket holes were round because they were drilled with rounded-nose

32a. Late 17th century dovetail

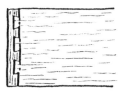

32b. Early / mid 18th century dovetails

32c. Late 18th / early 19th century dovetails

augers (fig. 34).

(e) Square or oblong (but never round) wooden pins that

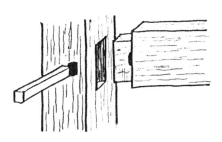

33. Mortise and tenon joint

have been squeezed (by shrinkage of the surrounding wood) out of their holes by at least 1/16th of an inch. These pins were usually ash, hickory, beech, or oak.

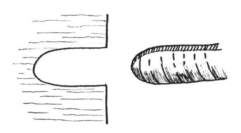

34. *Round mortise; spoon bit*

(f) Expect scribe marks (thin shallow grooves in the wood, not a pencil mark) made by an awl to be used as follows (figs. 32 and 35):

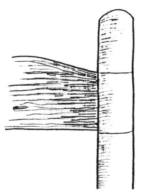

35. *Scribe lines*

(1) To designate where round furniture parts fit into sockets, such as a scribe mark around a chair leg.

(2) To designate the size and location of mortise

holes.

(3) To designate the location of dovetail cuts on a drawer.

(4) To designate where chair slats fit into back posts: usually 2 marks for each slat.

(5) To designate where a stretcher is attached to a table or chair leg.

(6) To designate on side stretchers of Windsor chairs where the center stretcher is to be socketed.

What You Should Not Expect Regarding Joints:

(a) The use of scalloped dovetails for drawers, which were used in the late 19th century (fig. 36).

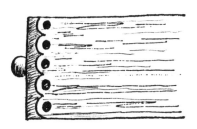

36. *Victorian scalloped dovetails*

(b) Machine-cut dovetails, which were used after the mid-19th century: uniform in appearance, short, and almost squarish-looking (fig. 37).

(c) Joints comprised of perfectly round dowels less than 1/2 inch long, which were not used in furniture before the Victorian era. A dowelled butt joint is a round wooden peg used to join 2 pieces of wood together; it is not a joint where 1 or 2 wooden pins

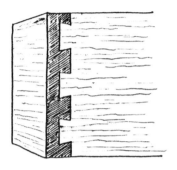

37. Machine-cut dovetails

are passed through a mortise and tenon to hold them together (fig. 38).

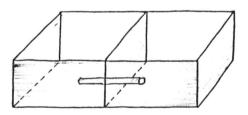

38. Dowelled butt joint

(d) Scribe marks made with a pencil.

(e) A mortise hole or socket hole that is flat-bottomed with a pit in the center, which is mid-19th century or later, because it was made by a modern gimlet-pointed bit (fig. 39).

39. Pointed mortise; modern gimlet-pointed bit

Hand Turning

Expect irregularities and marks as evidence that turned parts of furniture, such as legs and posts, were turned by hand.

What You Should Expect Regarding Turned Parts:

(a) Hand-turned parts should not have identical diameters. For instance, the thicknesses of the 6 legs of a period William and Mary highboy should not be the same when measured with calipers, nor should the thicknesses of a chair's finials.

(b) Marks of a turner's chisel may be visible on legs, posts, etc., as narrow gouges or slight ridges spiraling around the turning. They are usually more easily discernible on narrower turnings.

What You Should Not Expect Regarding Turned Parts:

Similar turned parts with identical diameters.

Molding, Beading, Inlay, and Reeding

What You Should Expect Regarding Hand-carved Molding, Beading, Inlay, and Reeding:

(a) Molding will appear uneven when sighted by eye.

(b) Moldings were hand-carved, not applied. For instance, the molding on a chair's knee bracket was carved from solid wood, has visible tool marks, and grain that continues through the molding. A carved shell should only be 1 piece of wood.

(c) Period beading was carved out of the wood; the grain should continue through it.

(d) Period cock-beading was glued.

(e) Because of shrinkage in the surrounding wood, genuine inlay will rise above the surface of that wood. Some inlay will buckle or appear uneven. If there is a scratch on either side of the inlay, it should continue through the inlay.

(f) Reeding or fluting will appear uneven when sighted by eye.

(g) Antique inlay will be hand cut and of high quality.

What You Should Not Expect Regarding Hand Molding, Beading, Inlay, and Reeding:

(a) If the beads were glued on, they were Victorian or later.

(b) If cock-beading was pinned, then the piece is Victorian or the beading is a later addition.

Veneer

What You Should Expect Regarding Veneer:

(a) Old veneer was thick, measuring from 1/16th to 1/8th of an inch.

(b) During the 18th century, veneer was usually applied to pine (or to deal in England), oak, or occasionally after 1750, mahogany.

(c) If drawer fronts are veneered, expect a veneered top.

(d) If an antique, such as a chest-on-chest, is entirely veneered, ascertain whether all holes used by earlier brasses continue through the veneer. If not, the veneer is not original to the piece.

What You Should Not Expect Regarding Veneer:

Veneer that is 1/32nd of an inch at the thickest, which would mean that the veneer is Victorian or later.

Worm Holes

What You Should Expect Regarding Worm Holes:

Real worm holes bend, are never the same size, and are normally not channels along the wood's surface.

What You Should Not Expect Regarding Worm Holes:

A wire or needle inserted into a worm hole to pass through the board or to travel a perfectly straight line, which would indicate that the hole is a fake.

Old Glass

What You Should Expect Regarding Old Glass:

Glass that is imperfect, slightly tinted (a grayish, bluish, or brownish tinge), wavy, and, perhaps, with a bull's eye. Try reading something through it.

What You Should Not Expect Regarding Old Glass:

Smooth glass, which was not made until the late 19th century.

Holes

What You Should Expect Regarding Holes:

An explicable reason for the existence of all holes found in a piece of furniture.

What You Should Not Expect Regarding Holes:

Any hole in a board with no explicable reason for it, which would indicate the board probably had a prior life. For example, if a hole in the lid of a chest fails to extend through the cleat, then the cleat is a replacement.

Wood

This manual merely touches upon a complex subject about which volumes have been written: the kinds of wood used in the 17th and 18th centuries to construct furniture in America and England. Wood is an important factor to help distinguish American from English furniture or colonial revival from 17th or 18th century furniture or to ascribe an antique to a particular region. This is especially true of secondary wood, because cabinetmakers were cost conscious and used indigenous wood for furniture parts that were not meant to be seen.

What You Should Expect Regarding Wood:

(a) In the 17th century, English oak and walnut were used as primary woods in England. Oak, walnut, and maple were used as primary woods in America.

(b) In the 18th century, walnut was used as a primary wood in both countries. After 1730, different varieties of mahogany were imported into both countries and used as primary wood. Maple, cherry, and birch were prevalent in America. After 1780, satinwood became popular, especially in England. Some woods served particular needs, such as beech (very scarce in American furniture), birch, and maple for legs of Windsor chairs. Hickory was also used in American Windsor chairs. Elm was used in

English Windsor chairs, especially for seats.

(c) In America, the most common secondary woods were white pine, yellow pine, and tulip poplar. Atlantic white cedar, spruce, chestnut, butternut, oak, and cypress were less commonly used secondary woods. In England, oak and deal (Scottish pine) were used extensively as secondary woods.

(d) Wood identification is extremely difficult. Self-help books with wood samples are available.

(e) Write to the following address for information about how to send a wood sample for microanalysis: Forest Products Laboratory, 1 Gifford Pinchot, Madison, WI 53705-2398.

What You Should Not Expect Regarding Wood:

Plywood as the back or bottom of a case piece because it is a 20th century invention.

Feel

Feel the antique. Comparable surfaces should feel the same. Do all finished surfaces feel the same? Do all unfinished surfaces feel the same? On unfinished wood, you should feel the saw marks. Old pins should not be flush. Strips of veneer should be slightly raised. The inside surfaces of a case piece should not feel smooth.

Consistency of Construction and Workmanship

Expect consistency of construction and workmanship in a genuine antique. Be especially thorough when examining 2-part antiques, such as a chest-on-chest, highboy, cupboard, or secretary (fig. 40).

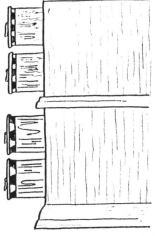

40. *2-part case with dissimilar dovetails*

Ask questions such as the following:

(a) Are all dovetails the same?

(b) Are all drawers constructed similarly?

(c) Are molding contours the same?

(d) Are the quality and workmanship of the carving consistent?

(e) Are design motifs consistent?

When examining a set of chairs, study them one-by-one to determine if they were made by the same person. Measure the distance between scribe lines on each chair. Comparable measurements should be the same for all chairs. Measure the width of each seat; the widths should be the same.

Wood Grain

What You Should Expect Regarding Wood Grain:

(a) The grain of wood on the same side of both parts of a 2-part antique should be the same.

(b) On a table, make sure that the grain runs through the full length of the pedestal or legs (fig. 41).

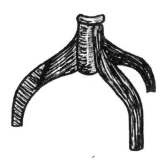

41. Spliced leg

(c) Until the mid-18th century, the grain of drawer bottoms ran front to back; after that it ran side to side.

(d) The grain should run through scribe marks, such as those used to mark dovetails on the sides of drawers; any break indicates that the drawer has been shortened or rebuilt (fig. 42).

(e) In the 17th and 18th centuries, veneer was applied with the grain running in the same direction as that of the wood beneath.

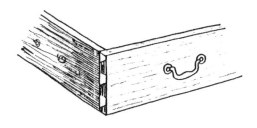

42. *Reworked drawer side*

(f) If a 17th or early 18th century antique has inlay set into veneered wood, the grain of the veneer should not continue through the inlay because a different piece of veneer would have been used on each side of it.

What You Should Not Expect Regarding Wood Grain:

(a) Different grain on the upper and lower parts of a 2-part antique.

(b) Grain that does not continue the full length of a leg or pedestal.

(c) Grain that differs on either side of a scribe mark.

(d) Grain of veneer that runs perpendicular to the grain of the wood beneath, which occurred during the Victorian era.

(e) Grain of veneer that continues through the inlay, which would indicate that the inlay was a later addition.

CHAPTER 6. EXAMINATION OF PARTICULAR PARTS OF ANTIQUE FURNITURE

This chapter focuses on key parts of various antique furniture forms as a means of detecting replacements, repairs, or renovations which may have a profound negative impact on market value. The parts discussed below were chosen because they are quite susceptible to damage and subsequent repair, replacement, or enhancement. Drawers were used and reused until they wore out. Tabletops suffered from heavy usage and abuse. Legs were damaged and replaced or spliced. Feet rotted and were knocked about.

Drawers

(a) Are the drawers original? Remove each drawer and examine every surface of every drawer. You should expect to find the following:

   (1) All drawers should be constructed in the same manner:

      (A) The shape of dovetails and manner of joining bottoms to sides and backs should be the same.

      (B) Drawer fronts of the same wood with similar wood grain and of the same thickness.

      (C) Drawer sides, backs, and bottoms made from the same secondary woods and of the same thicknesses as each other.

      (D) Top edges of the sides of all drawers the

same shape.

(2) The method of construction used to build a drawer should be a method used when it was supposedly made:

(A) In the mid-17th century, drawers were lap-jointed and nailed, and had thick sides because they were "hung" drawers. A groove was cut into each side of a drawer and this moved along a runner built inside the case (fig. 43).

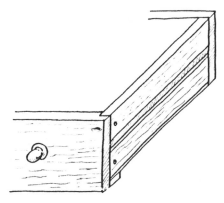

43. 17th century hung drawer

(B) From about 1690 through the early 19th century, most drawers were held together by hand-cut dovetails. As a rule of thumb, expect the following: one large dovetail in drawers from the late 17th century; 1 or 2 wide (usually from 2 to 4 inches), stubby, crude dovetails in the early 18th century; 2 or 3 narrower, but still wide, stubby, dovetails in the second and third quarters of the

18th century; and 4 or 5 thin and fragile looking dovetails in the fourth quarter of the 18th century and the first quarter of the 19th century (fig. 44).

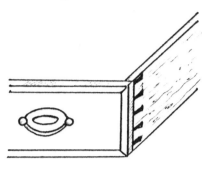

44. *Late 18th / early 19th century drawer*

(C) From the late 17th to the mid-19th century, many country-made drawers were rabetted and nailed together.

(3) Expect evidence of wear on a drawer bottom that corresponds to the surfaces it slides across. If a divider has been repaired and a drawer bottom has not, the drawer was not original to that antique, because the divider is usually made of a harder wood than the drawer that slides across it. Normally, wear on a drawer bottom is in the form of a concave line.

(4) The color of the sides, bottom, and back of a drawer should be relatively light and uniform.

(5) Marks for the present and/or original brasses consistent on the inside and outside of drawer fronts, including the distance between any empty holes left by any removed brasses.

(6) A drawer should have patina where it was touched to open or close it. A keyhole should have patina and nicks adjacent to it.

(7) American drawers were usually pine or tulip poplar, perhaps chestnut, rarely oak. English drawers were usually oak.

(8) The drawer bottom should usually be one board, fairly thick, and chamfered around the edges (fig. 45).

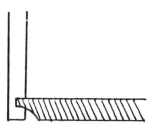

45. *Chamfered drawer bottom*

In the 17th and early 18th centuries, bottoms ran front to back (fig. 46). From the mid-18th century, bottoms ran side to side (fig. 47). In the late 18th and early 19th centuries in England muntin partitions were used on bottoms and quarter-round moldings were glued along a drawer's interior edges (fig. 48).

(9) There should be about a 2-inch gap between the drawer and back of the case for air circulation. If the drawer touches the back or is too short, be suspicious.

(10) A drawer should be properly balanced. If you pull out a drawer and it is front-heavy, it has probably been cut down.

46.   Drawer bottom front to back

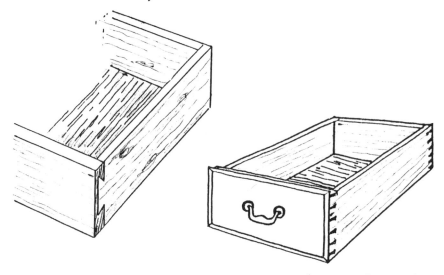

47.   Drawer bottom side to side

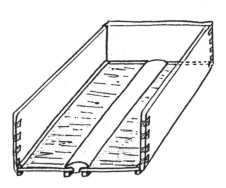

48.   Late 18th / early 19th century English drawer

(11) If there is a scratch on the outside of a drawer side, the inside of the case should have a nail or similar object that could have caused the scratch. If not, the drawer may have come from another piece or the side may be a replacement.

(b) You should not expect to find the following:

(1) Any evidence of paint, varnish, or stain on the inside or outside of any drawer (except the finished drawer front), because unexposed drawer surfaces were not finished and it would only be done to hide newer wood or reworking of old wood.

(2) A glue line around the outer edges of the drawer fronts, which may indicate new drawer fronts.

Tabletops

(a) Examine the top and then turn it over and ask the following questions:

(1) What is its condition? Look for wear and possible warpage or splitting. Expect edges and corners to be rounded from wear, not sharp or pristine. Expect wear on a leaf caused by a swinging support leg. The surface of an 18th century table should show subtle nuances because it was hand-planed.

(2) If the top is square or rectangular, check the edges for holes, which may indicate that it had been a floorboard.

(3) If you remove the top, can you can see the shadow of the old frame on the underside of the top? If not, the top is a replacement.

(4) Has the underside been completely finished or painted? If so, it is a fake.

(5) After removing the drawer (if any), is the

underside of the top that was protected by the drawer lighter than the surrounding wood? It should be. Does wear on the underside of the drawer bottom conform to the drawer supports? It should.

(6) If the top of the table is round, is there shrinkage across its grain? If so, you know the top has age, but you do not know if it belongs with the base or was made in the 17th or 18th century.

(7) Was the top made from one board? A 17th or 18th century top less than 3-feet wide was usually cut from one board.

(b) The following specialized facts may be useful:

(1) It was very common for a faker to enhance a tilt-top table by adding a scalloped (pie-crust) border. Be sure that all carving is original to the piece. Any cracks in the wood surface should continue through the carving.

(2) Plugged screw holes along the underside of a circular top may indicate that the top is a reconverted Victorian table that had an apron.

(3) If a top appears too thick for its size, it may have been reduced.

(4) On a country table, the top may have been turned over years ago because of wear or made from a cutting board.

Pedestals

(a) Tilt the tabletop. The top of the pedestal ends in a block of wood. The wear marks on the underside of the tilt top and on the block should be identical (fig. 49). Otherwise, the top and the pedestal are not original to each other. The underside of the top where it rests on the block should be lighter than the rest of the underside. Old pole screens or torcheres may be cut-down and circular tops attached to form a married tilt-top table. Examine the joining of the top and the pedestal for anything suspect such as stain or evidence of a disturbed surface.

(b) The block at the top of the pedestal should either be hinged to cleats that are screwed to the top or screwed directly into the top.

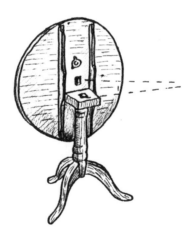

49. Consistent wear marks

(c) If the block is mahogany, the table is probably English.

(d) The 3 legs should be dovetailed into the bottom of the pedestal and, usually, a triangular-shaped iron brace is attached there to provide additional support.

Legs

(a) In the case of turned legs, examine them as follows:

(1) Study all scribe marks carefully. A scribe line served as a measuring point to allow a turner to drill deep mortises on 2 sides of a leg for stretchers and not have the holes intersect. A front stretcher might be set just below the scribe line and a side stretcher just above it. If the 2 stretchers are at the same height, then the mortises could not be deep enough and the chair is not a period piece.

(2) Follow the grain of the wood to be sure that it does not change, especially at a scribe line. A change would indicate a spliced leg.

(3) Study any paint on each turned part (especially where paint removal would be difficult) for a consistent paint history. If a certain color appears on one leg and not another, then one is a replacement.

(4) Expect a pattern between turnings on front and back posts. If none exists, the chair may be made of old parts of various antiques.

(5) On a high-back, turned chair, if the front legs are too slender, the antique may be a late 19th century colonial revival chair.

(b) If a chair or table has cabriole legs, check for a replaced leg by comparing the 2 front legs from a distance. If the curves are not identical, one leg is a replacement.

(c) If a table has a swing leg, it should show more wear than the stationary legs, both where it scrapes the top as it is swung and under its foot.

(d) If a chair has rockers, are they original? Any rockers on a colonial chair are an addition, because they were not invented until the late 18th century. Compare the paint history of the rockers to the rest of the chair. If the rockers are a later addition, the rungs are usually too close to the bottom of the feet. On original rockers the distance between the bottom of the front rung and the bottom of the front leg is approximately 3 1/2 inches; the distance from a side rung to the floor is approximately 5 to 5 1/2 inches. Late 18th and very early 19th century rocking chairs are rare: rockers extend about the same distance from the front and rear legs of the chair, are taller than they are wide, and were mortised and pinned into the legs. After that, rockers became longer in the rear than in the front and the legs were socketed into the rockers instead of rockers mortised into the legs.

Feet

(a) Expect feet to be in fairly bad shape, due to dampness, dragging, and general wear. Feet are the most common replacements on antique furniture.

(b) Turned feet are dowelled into the bottom of a case and bracket feet are usually glued in place. Both are quite vulnerable.

(c) Look for saw and rasp marks on support blocks and foot brackets.

(d) Stained support blocks are replacements.

(e) If carving lacks definition, such as poor toes on ball and claw feet, the antique may be a late 19th century colonial revival piece.

Arms

(a) Check to see if arm supports are screwed to a seat rail with modern screws.

(b) Beware of an armchair with a seat only as wide as a side chair, because it is probably a side chair with arms added.

(c) If permissible, remove the arms, the wood underneath the arm supports should be unfinished. If the wood is finished, the arm support is not original to the chair.

(d) An arm of a Chippendale chair or settee that terminates in a bird's head is usually an enhancement. Many were added to legitimate antiques in the 1920s and 1930s.

CHAPTER 7. EXAMINATION OF MAJOR FURNITURE FORMS

This chapter applies the factors discussed in chapter 5, such as wood grain, history of brasses, tool marks, patina, paint history, and wood shrinkage, to particular furniture forms to determine whether a particular piece of furniture is a genuine antique, extensively repaired, or a fake.

Chairs

(a) Are the legs original? Compare tool marks, wear, color, and paint history. Check for shrinkage. Are any turned legs slightly out of round? If a leg is square does it have shrinkage across the grain? Have any legs have been spliced? Look for splices, differences in wood grain, or differences in color, especially at a scribe line or narrow turning. Examine the bottom of each foot for a dowel that might attach a new foot to the leg.

(b) Are the feet original? Look for wear and proper patina.

(c) Are the stretchers original? Compare tool marks, wear, color, and paint history. On the front stretcher, the outside upper edge should be more heavily worn than the inside upper edge and the center should not show as much wear as where shoes would have rested. The inside lower edge of that stretcher should show no wear. Center stretchers were mortised or dovetailed into side stretchers. Side stretchers were mortised into the legs and flush with the outside of the legs.

(d) Is the seat original?

(1) From the top of the seat to the floor should be 17 to 18 inches. If it is less, the chair has lost some original height (fig. 50).

(2) The seat of an armchair should be about 2 inches wider than the seat of a side chair.

(3) If the seat is a plank-seat, it should be made from one board and show hand-planing marks underneath.

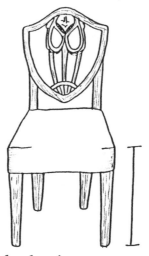

50. Seat height of 17 to 18 inches

(4) Has a splint seat replaced a rush seat? Rush seats leave many parallel, narrow impressions on the seat rails. Spread the splints apart to look for these indentations.

(5) Do not expect unexposed seat rails on rush or splint-seated chairs to be turned or have sharp edges or be finished or made from an expensive wood. The rails should be shaped like a blade (but worn from wear, with no sharp edges), unfinished, and made from inexpensive, local wood.

(6) A seat rail can either be above the front legs and attached by a rectangular mortise and tenon or attached to the inside of each front leg by a round mortise and tenon joint. But the round tenon will not be perfectly round and the mortise will not be made from a modern drill bit.

(e) Are the arms original? Compare tool marks, wear, color, and paint history. Look for evidence of new saw cuts to discover if the arms have been replaced. Replaced wood in the back posts above or below the arms would indicate this. Expect the same patination on the underside of both arms of an armchair. An arm upright was attached to a seat rail by 2 screws and an arm was attached to the side of a back leg with 1 screw. In 18th century America, screws were generally used from the inside out. There would be no wooden plug to cover the screw head. In 18th century England, holes were drilled and screws were countersunk below the surface and then plugged with wood. The screws are not visible. If a chair is genuine, wooden plugs will have blended with the surrounding surface and not be discernable. If you see wooden plugs, then either the arms have been added or the chair is Victorian or later.

(f) Are the banisters, slats, splat, and crest rail original? Slats or banisters should be similar thickness and color and be made from the same wood. Pins used to secure them should be the same size and shape. There should be no depth of carving on the back of a crest rail of a late 17th or 18th century high-back chair.

(g) Does the wear or lack of wear make sense?

(h) Has the chair been repainted?

(i) Does the chair have tool marks and other evidence of being hand-made? Expect scribe marks where parts are mortised or joined together and socket holes with rounded ends (indicating the use of a pod auger). Check the shape of holes with a pocket knife.

(j) If there is worm damage, are there tiny holes and not channels parallel to the surface of the wood?

(k) Are there too many unrelated motifs (a lack of overall design)? If so, the chair may have been enhanced.

(l) Are the corner blocks original? The two-piece quarter-round corner block was glued; the one-piece, triangular corner block was glued and nailed or screwed; and the open corner block was glued and/or screwed (figs. 51a, 51b, and 51c).

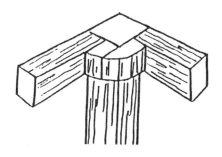

51a. Quarter-round corner block

Be wary of disturbed surfaces, uneven patina, new cuts, new screws or nails, or lack of hand tool markings. It is quite common for corner blocks to have been lost and replaced.

(m) A finial or mushroom handhold should be made from the post it forms the top of.

51b. Triangular corner block

51c. Open corner block

(n) The seat rails should match each other and have the same patina.

(o) Be suspicious of a chair that is refinished with thick, dark varnish that may obscure modifications.

(p) Carving on the knee of a Queen Anne or Chippendale cabriole leg should project above the surface of the rest of the leg (fig. 52a). If it does not, the carving is probably a later improvement (fig. 52b). As a general rule, areas of lower relief should be crisp and undamaged. But carving that projects the farthest above the surrounding wood should be smooth from wear.

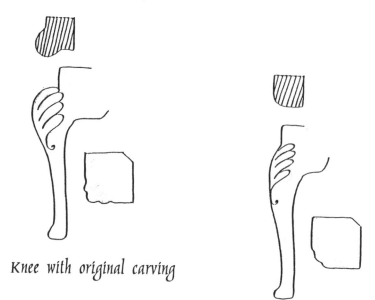

52a.   Knee with original carving

52b.   Knee with later carving

Look for patination around old carving. Cracks or dents adjacent to carving should continue across the carving.

Windsor Chairs

(a) Do all parts have the same paint history? Examine where parts join, narrow turnings, seat bottoms, and at scribe marks. Green, black, red, and white were the most commonly used paint colors in the 18th and early 19th centuries.

(b) Does the chair have the shrinkage expected of an old chair? Spindles should protrude through the crest rail and legs should protrude through the seat.

(c) Is the seat original? It should be one piece of wood

about 2 inches thick at its thickest. There should be shallow grooves parallel to the grain underneath the seat, which indicates hand planing. Check along its outer edges for evidence of new saw cuts. Check for evidence of new planing to improve the shape of the seat.

(d) Have the legs been spliced or replaced? Make sure that the legs are the same color as each other and have the same wood on each side of each ring turning.

(e) If the legs protrude through the seat, do the tops of the legs seem about as worn as the surrounding seat? They should show less wear, but some wear.

(f) Are the spindles correct? Feel each spindle to ascertain whether they feel the same as each other. Try to twist each spindle to see if it is made from one piece of wood. Compare the tops of all of the spindles to see if they appear to be the same or if any appear to be new. If there is a bend in a spindle above where it passes through a part of the chair different from most of the other spindles, the spindle may be new.

(g) Are there any new saw cuts where the arm supports penetrate the seat, replaced wedges, or extra holes indicating a possible replacement?

(h) Has the chair been improved? Carving on knuckle handholds, if any, should appear as old as other carving on the chair. Check for evidence that the comb is new or that the ears, if any, have been improved.

(i) Factory made, low-back Windsors referred to as Firehouse Windsors or captain's chairs were made beginning in the mid-19th century.

Upholstered Chairs and Sofas

(a) Expect the frame to be held together by mortise and tenon joints, not round dowels, unless a later repair.

(b) Expect evidence, in the form of upholstery tack holes, of many reupholsterings.

(c) Examine upholstery tack holes in the seat frame, crest rail, and arms to be sure they were each reupholstered the same number of times.

(d) Examine the legs to ascertain if they have been spliced or replaced.

(e) Beware of any staining on the crest rail to hide reshaping.

(f) Stretchers were mortised into the legs. Beware of perfectly round wooden dowels. Compare the patina of the stretcher to the patina of other exposed wood. Check for logical wear.

(g) The back legs of wing chairs were made of hardwood and spliced onto soft wood. Feel the splice to be sure that the soft wood has pulled away from the hardwood. It should because the soft wood will have dried out more and therefore have shrunk more.

Tall Case Pieces: Secretaries, Highboys, and Chests-on-chests

The most likely replacements are feet and slant-front lids. Central doors are vulnerable. Desk interiors may be replaced or improved, cornices enhanced, and tops reshaped. The comments made below regarding a 2-part secretary would apply equally to a 2-part highboy or chest-on-chest.

(a) On a 2-part secretary, is the piece married? Many desks were not made with bookcases. If the desk and the bookcase are original to each other, expect the following:

(1) A top board on the desk that is unfinished, with exposed dovetails at both ends, nail-hole evidence of moldings around its front and sides (if the molding is missing), and no overhang in the back.

(2) Backs on both parts of the same wood and color.

(3) Identical hardware or evidence of previous hardware.

(4) The same evidence of wormholes on boards of the same wood.

(5) Consistent workmanship, such as identical drawer dovetailing or other manner of joining for all drawers.

(6) Identical wood thickness when comparing comparable boards, such as the sides of each part.

(7) A bookcase that is about half the depth of the desk, 1 1/2 to 3 inches narrower, and taller than the desk. If a desk's top board is finished and of the same wood as its sides, then the bookcase is a later addition.

(b) Is the slant-front lid original? If so, expect the following:

(1) A lid and desk of the same wood.

(2) Molded outer edges.

(3) Consistent hinge marks on the lid and desk.

(4) A lock (if any) on the lid that matches the lock plate on the desk.

(5) The inside surface of a desk lid should have wear, such as scratch marks and ink spots.

(c) Is any inlay on the lid not original? This will be difficult to ascertain unless the quality of workmanship on the lid differs considerably from the rest of the piece.

(d) Are the wood slides that support the slant-front lid original or have they been replaced? Check to see if they have the same finish and if the edges and ends exhibit comparable wear.

(e) If the desk has interior drawers, they should fit upside down as well as right side up.

(f) Do the construction methods and quality of the interior and of the desk match?

(g) In the case of a highboy or chest-on-chest, beware of these additional considerations:

(1) Is the bonnet top original? Look for new saw cuts, any inexplicable change in the patina on its top or back, or any staining to cover-up changes.

(2) Has the skirt been reshaped? Look for new saw cuts, disturbance of patina, or staining that would indicate reshaping.

(3) Are the finials and pendants original? Look for wear and marks produced by hand-chiseling. Be sure that each finial or pendant is one piece of wood.

Cupboards

(a) In the case of one-part cupboards (other than corner cupboards), each side should be made from one board. More than one board may indicate a fake or considerable restoration.

(b) In the case of 2-part cupboards, expect the following:

(1) Backboards with the same patina and finished in the same manner.

(2) Sides, backboards, tops, and bottoms from the same piece of wood.

(3) The same paint history on both parts.

(4) The same construction methods and decorative elements on the 2 parts.

(c) In the case of cupboards without doors, was the piece originally made with doors? Are there any empty hinge mortises or any that have been patched?

(d) In the case of cupboards with doors, are the doors authentic? Expect the following if the doors are original:

(1) A paint history on the doors that is consistent with each other and the rest of the cupboard.

(2) Backs of doors that feel like they were finished in the same manner as the inside sides of the cupboard.

(3) If there is a latch or indication of one on the inside of any door, then a matching slot under the appropriate shelf.

(4) If the door has glass panes, expect at least some panes of old glass and muntins aligned with the shelves' edges. If not, perhaps the doors are not original or blind

panels have been replaced by panes of glass.

(5) The same beading or molding on top and bottom doors.

(6) Hinge marks and mortises for hinges consistent on the door and the cupboard.

(e) Are there any new saw cuts? If the edge of the cut shows "feathers", or is fresh or stained, then the cut is recent.

Chests of Drawers

(a) Are the drawers original? Turn to the checklist for drawers in chapter 6.

(b) Are the feet original? They should show proper wear and patination where they rub the floor. Ball feet should be slightly elliptical.

(c) Is the color of the wood inside the piece consistent, such as where the bottom meets the sides? Look carefully for evidence of refinishing to artificially attain a consistent color.

(d) Is the top original? If so, expect the following: a top made of one piece of wood with its back edge the same color as the backboards, which shows it was not old timber cut down.

Beware of the following indicators of an inappropriate top for a chest of drawers: a top with exposed dovetails, molding attached only along its edge, and made of a secondary wood, which may be a chest of drawers made from the upper part of a chest-on-chest; or an overhang that is too large, which could indicate a chest made from a highboy.

(e) Do the backboards match each other in color,

workmanship, nails utilized, joints, type of finish, and feel? This is very important on pieces with separate upper and lower cases. Remember, backboards should not be painted, varnished, or stained, which would be done to hide replacement boards or new sawcuts. There should be space between the boards caused by shrinkage. Be wary of inexplicable, empty nail holes. The back should neither be one piece of wood, nor be plywood (a 20th century invention). Carefully examine all edges (top, bottom, and sides) of backboards for evidence of replaced boards. The edges should not be stained, a lighter color, or "feathered".

(f) Is there new carving to improve the chest, such as the addition of a shell?

(g) Is the molding original? It should exhibit the unmistakable marks of planing by hand and be secured with brads or pins.

(h) The following specialized facts may prove useful:

(1) If a tall chest does not appear tall enough, has too strong a cornice, and has the drawer configuration usually found in a highboy, then it is probably the divorced top of an erstwhile highboy.

(2) If a lowboy is too tall (more than 30 inches) and larger than the "normal sized" lowboy, it could be the lower half of a highboy with a replaced top.

(3) For a William and Mary high chest, expect the following:

(A) The outline of the stretchers to echo the outline of the skirt.

(B) Uniform color on its underside.

(C) Visible dovetails joining its back and sides.

(D) Replaced legs and feet if the stretchers have been replaced.

(4) If the overhang (depth) of each part of a two-part corner cupboard is different, assume the piece is "married."

Tables

(a) Is the top original? The following may indicate a replaced top:

(1) Empty holes that are inexplicable.

(2) Difference in color between underside of top and inside of the table frame.

(3) New saw cuts or "feathered" edges.

(4) Lack of wear along its edges.

(5) Refinishing of underside of top.

(6) Wear on the underside of top within the frame of the table.

(7) Boards of different coloration.

(8) A shadow outline underneath the top made by being affixed to another table frame.

(9) No hand planing marks.

(10) Different paint history from the other parts of the table.

(b) Are the leaves original? If so, you should expect to find the following:

(1) Single boards.

(2) Planing marks on the underside of the leaves that feel the same as those on the underside of the central top.

(3) Hand-made joints securing the top and the leaves.

(4) The same color on the underside of the leaves as the underside of the central top, especially where they meet.

(5) Wear marks under the leaves consistent with the supporting structure.

(6) Hinge mortises and nail or screw holes the same on the leaves as on the central top.

(c) Are the legs original? If so, you should expect to find the following:

(1) Legs attached to the frame and stretchers attached to legs by wooden pins that are tight fitting, slightly projecting, and not perfectly round.

(2) Turned legs slightly out of round.

(3) Scribe marks on the legs indicating where the mortise fits into the frame and where stretchers join legs.

(4) Feet with wear and patination.

(d) Do the stretchers (if any) have logical wear? The stretcher on the back of the table across from its drawers was often less worn than the front stretcher.

(e) If the table has drawers, see the checklist for drawers in chapter 6.

(f) The following specialized facts may prove useful:

(1) Some period (mid-17th to mid-19th century) tavern tables have removable tops. Expect tavern table tops to exhibit extreme wear. The ends of the legs should protrude through the top.

(2) Period (early 18th century) butterfly tables are extremely rare and often faked. Many in curly maple were faked earlier this century. Expect uneven wear on side stretchers of a butterfly table because the leaf supports would have obstructed wear at the center of these stretchers. If side stretchers are old, but wear is even, the stretchers may have come from an old tavern table.

(3) On a period (mid-17th through the end of the 18th century) gateleg table, the top and each of the 2 leaves should be a single board.

(4) A period (mid-17th to mid-19th century) trestle table or sawbuck table is not permanently joined and may be taken apart by removing the pegs or wedges that hold it together. Later tables are usually permanently joined, shorter, and have multiple-board tops.

(5) In the case of a pedestal dining table the following: no inlay on its top; at least 6 inches of patination on the underside of its top; no sharp edges on its legs; and, if the edge of the top is plain, the legs will be plain; if the edge is reeded, the legs will be reeded.

(6) Most Sheraton drum tables are converted Victorian ones. If its drawers are narrower at the back than the front, the table has been tampered with.

(7) A pair of card tables is very valuable. If they

are a pair, they should look alike underneath.

(8) A game table will rarely have a drawer. Therefore any game table drawer should be carefully examined to be certain that it is original to the table.

Beds

(a) Expect the feet to show appropriate wear and patination underneath and, perhaps, to be decayed from exposure to moisture.

(b) Expect posts to be hand turned, out of round, show irregularities of hand workmanship, and be at least 3 inches in diameter where joined to the frame. Look on the insides of the posts for evidence of earlier tenons. Check for piecing or splicing. Many bulky Empire beds were made into more salable Sheraton and Hepplewhite beds.

(c) Check the posts, rails, headboard, and footboard for new saw cuts, piecing, or splicing, and for an identical paint history.

(d) If Roman numerals were carved into each part of the bed, were all such Roman numerals carved by the same person? They should have been.

(e) Each post should be turned from one piece of wood.

Mirrors

(a) Replaced modern glass greatly reduces the value of a mirror. Original glass is wavy, uneven, dull, and usually has a bluish cast.

(b) Look for modern nails or extra holes that hold the wooden back to the frame of the mirror and may indicate tampering.

(c) Expect patination on the wooden back of a mirror; the wood color is usually darker at the top.

(d) Old mirror glass is very thin. Hold a silver coin against the surface of the mirror; the distance between the coin and its reflection is the thickness of the glass. Do this with a reproduction mirror to compare the difference; the reproduction glass will appear much thicker.

(e) Silvering on old glass is usually foggy or missing in several places.

(f) A Queen Anne period mirror is bevelled and the line of demarcation between the bevel and the face of the glass is very subtle.

Stools

(a) Genuine period 17th and 18th century stools are extremely rare.

(b) Many are made out of chairs. If the underside of a seat rail has a Roman numeral carved into it, it was made from a chair from a set.

(c) Rounded corners usually indicate that a stool was made from a chair.

(d) Expect patination where it would be handled.

CHAPTER 8. CASE STUDIES IN THE FIELD

Case No. 1

You are considering the purchase of a set of formal dining room chairs. A dealer is selling 4 "period Chippendale mahogany side chairs, with pierced splats and ball and claw feet, circa 1770."

Stand back and study the 4 chairs. Are they a set? Are the same primary and secondary woods used on each of the chairs? Examination reveals that the chairs are all made of mahogany and of the same secondary wood. Measure the seat heights and dimensions to be sure they are the same. A measurement confirms that they are. Stand in front of the chairs to compare the actual curves of their front legs. The curves are identical; therefore, none of the legs appears to be a replacement.

Next, study each chair. A close examination of each leg shows that the grain continues throughout and there are no splices. Flip the chair over. The bottom of the feet are very close-grained, with score marks, and quite smooth. This is the patination you would expect.

Look under the seat of each chair. With 1 or 2 exceptions, the corner blocks are the 2-piece quarter round blocks that were found on some 18th century chairs. They appear undisturbed. Neither the blocks nor the surrounding wood have been finished or stained, which indicates no tampering. The patination is correct. The wood looks old and has similar ageing. A few replaced blocks appear newer and are secured with modern gimlet screws. This is to be expected. There are similar hand tool marks on all of the chairs.

Before you make an offer, determine whether the chairs are American or English. American chairs are much more valuable. The only secondary wood used in their construction is oak, therefore, assume the chairs are English. The price should reflect this.

Case No. 2

You are in an antique shop trying to decide whether to buy 1 of 2 "mahogany tilt-top tables, circa 1770-1790".

You measure the diameter of table #1 with the grain and across the grain. The measurements are identical. Since you know that wood shrinks across the grain, the top is not from the 18th century; it is not even 100 years old. Also, the top is made from 3 pieces of wood, which would not have been done in the 18th century. Next, you measure the pedestal with a pair of calipers and find that it has one-quarter inch of shrinkage. That means that the pedestal is at least 100 years old. The plate at the top of the pedestal usually scars the underside of the top. As you expected by this time, the scars on the plate and on the underside of the top do not match. This is further proof that the base and the top are not original to each other. For obvious reasons, you decide against this piece. The antique is not even a marriage of 2 old parts because the top is new. Its fair market value is reduced by about 80 percent.

A similar examination of the second tilt-top table reveals that all parts are antique and original to each other, but the grain of one of the legs does not continue through to its foot. The leg was spliced and the foot is a replacement. The quality of the replacement is good. The replacement produces about a 20 percent reduction in the fair market value of the table. If you are still interested in buying the table, negotiate. Perhaps the dealer will reduce the asking price by significantly more than 20 percent and you will have a nice table with a repair that is not terribly noticeable.

Case No. 3

You are in a private home considering the purchase of a purported early 19th century 2-part walnut Hepplewhite secretary. Stand back and look at the piece. Is the piece English or American? Are the proportions correct? Are the bookcase and desk stylistically the same? Was the same wood used to construct both parts? An examination reveals that the desk's side board is thicker than the bookcase's side board. When viewed from behind, the patination of the backboards on the 2 parts is dissimilar. One is significantly darker than the other.

If you are uninterested in buying a married piece, the examination is over. If you would consider buying it at a good price if both parts are from the early 19th century, then continue the examination. Further study reveals that there is a difference in the darkening of both sets of backboards. The boards have experienced different climatic conditions. But both appear to have sufficient age. None of the boards have circular saw marks. They appear to have been hand cut and planed. There are gaps between the backboards due to shrinkage.

A close look at the desk reveals that its slant-front lid has had its hinges replaced. There is evidence of an earlier set of hinges. The lid itself has the appropriate shrinkage. It is a single board (as it should be) with breadboard ends that are now about one-quarter of an inch longer than the width of the board between them. This is because that board has shrunk across its grain. All of the drawers are held together by slender, hand-cut dovetails, which is to be expected in the early 19th century. The shaping of the dovetails on all drawers matches. The patination of the interior of the drawers is uniform and much lighter in color than the exterior of the backboards. None of the drawers have been spliced. The history of brasses on the exterior drawers is the same. Each has an additional 2 holes. The widths between each of those sets of holes is identical.

Remove all of the drawers. The patination on the inside of the case is a uniform, light brown color. There is no evidence of recent saw cuts or glue. There is no stain to hide repairs or restoration. Comparing the wear on the bottom of each side of each drawer to the wear on the divider that supports it reveals consistent wear. The drawers appear to be original to the case. Flip the desk onto its back and examine its feet and underside. With the exception of one front foot, the patination is uniform. The interior of this splay foot is stained and the glue blocks are attached by modern gimlet screws. This foot is a replacement.

Next, examine the bookcase. Some of the glass has a bluish tinge and appears wavy; the rest is clear. The former is old glass; the latter is new. You expect some replaced panes. Study the top of the bookcase. There are undisturbed, old glue blocks. There is no evidence of new saw cuts. The patination is quite dark and uniform.

The primary wood on both parts of the secretary is walnut, which could be either English walnut or American black walnut. The secondary wood appears to be gum, which is an American wood. This was ascertained by comparing the wood to a book of wood samples. To be absolutely certain, you would have the wood analyzed in a laboratory.

Do you want to purchase a married American Hepplewhite secretary with a replaced front foot? The value of this piece is diminished by between 50 and 75 percent from its otherwise fair market value. If you are still interested, make an offer that reflects this lower value.

CHAPTER 9. CONCLUSION

"I once remarked to furniture historian Colin Streeter how unusual it was that Luke Vincent Lockwood, Wallace Nutting, Percy McQuoid, and R.W. Symonds, fine connoisseurs all, could have been gulled into publishing, as antique, furniture that could not have been more than fifteen or twenty years old. 'Ah,' he responded, 'but they were taken in by the forgeries that were made for their generation.' Undoubtedly, future generations will find that we have been taken in by the forgeries that were made in our honor. The principle that emerges from this is that it is hard to think beyond the limits of one's own time."

-- Benno M. Forman
("American Seating Furniture
1630-1730" (1988))

Collecting antiques is a fascinating and unique endeavor because, to be a successful collector, one must master the three elements of collecting: the intellectual, aesthetic, and economic. This manual is about the first element: the intellectual.

Knowledge of antiques is essential before buying any because of the prevalence of fakes in the marketplace. As the above quotation states, many expert collectors have been fooled by good forgeries made for their generation. Why? Unfortunately, knowledge of style and construction alone are necessary but insufficient to enable a collector to distinguish fake from authentic. A good faker will construct a piece of furniture by hand using old techniques and the stylistic features will be correct. Yet the piece is not of the period.

What fakes are earmarked for today's generation of collectors? Perhaps 19th century painted country furniture, a current favorite, sought after by decorators and young collectors. How many of those faded blue rustic case pieces offered at auction have boards with "feathered" edges (indicative of recent saw cuts), inexplicable wear (indicative of reused old boards), dust evenly applied throughout their interiors (indicative of using an aerosol), or other indications of mischief? The seasoned faker knows his market.

After establishing an antique's authenticity and before buying it, consider the second element of collecting, the aesthetic. How great is its artistic merit? Is it commonplace among antiques of its genre or desirable? Is it well executed? These are difficult questions to answer, but they must be addressed.

As your knowledge of antiques increases, your taste should become more refined, your eyes more perceptive and critical, and your understanding and appreciation of early furniture makers' achievements more exacting. You will not expect the same from a country furniture maker as an urban furniture maker. But you will appreciate the aesthetic qualities of each.

There is no substitute for experience in mastering the aesthetic. You should visit historical collections, obtain and study catalogues of museum exhibits throughout the country, and read illustrated articles in publications such as *The Magazine Antiques.*

The third element of collecting to consider is the economic. What is an appropriate price to pay for a given antique? No book can answer this question. The market is too complex; prices are always changing. Read current price guides, attend auctions, visit numerous antique shops, and read advertisements and articles about auctions and important estate sales in publications such as the *Maine Antique Digest*.

To be a successful collector, you must continue your education, refine your aesthetic taste, and study the economic aspects of the antiques marketplace.

The words "caveat emptor" (let the buyer beware) are too often ignored by buyers of antiques. Restore them to your vocabulary. Dealers and auction houses buy and sell objects to make a profit. As collectors, you must discern whether these objects are what they are purported to be. If this manual assists in that endeavor and makes you more cautious and less trusting, more discerning and less gullible, then the manual is serving its purpose. Collecting is fun and interesting, but will always remain challenging and perplexing. You should now understand what it means to assume nothing when buying antiques!

SUGGESTED READINGS

Bishop, Robert. *How to Know American Antique Furniture.* New York: E.P. Dutton, 1973.

Boston Furniture of the Eighteenth Century. Edited by Walter Muir Whitehill, Brock Jobe, and Jonathan Fairbanks. Boston: Colonial Society of Massachusetts, 1974.

Burton, E. Milby. *Charleston Furniture, 1700-1825.* Charleston, S.C.: The Charleston Museum, 1955.

Cescinsky, Herbert. *The Gentle Art of Faking Furniture.* London, 1931. Reprint. New York: Dover Publications, 1967.

_____. *English Furniture from Gothic to Sheraton.* New York, 1937. Reprint. New York: Dover Publications, 1968.

Chinnery, Victor. *Oak Furniture; The British Tradition.* Woodbridge, Suffolk: Baron Publishing, 1979.

Comstock, Helen, ed. *The Concise Encyclopedia of American Antiques.* New York: Hawthorn Publishers, Inc., 1984.

Downs, Joseph. *American Furniture in the Winterthur Museum.* New York: MacMillan Publishing Company, 1952.

_____. *American Furniture: Queen Anne and Chippendale Periods.* New York: Bonanza Books, 1952.

Fales, Dean A., Jr. *American Painted Furniture, 1660-1880.* New York: E.P. Dutton, 1979.

Forman, Benno M., *American Seating Furniture 1630-1730.* New York and London: W.W. Norton & Company, 1988.

Gusler, Wallace B. *Furniture of Williamsburg and Eastern Virginia, 1710-1790.* Richmond, VA: Virginia Museum, 1979.

Heckscher, Morrison H. *American Furniture in the Metropolitan Museum of Art, II, Late Colonial Period: The Queen Anne and Chippendale Styles.* New York: The Metropolitan Museum of Art and Random House, 1986.

Hornor, William MacPherson, Jr. *Blue Book of Philadelphia Furniture.* Philadelphia: Graphic Arts Engraving Co., 1935.

Kirk, John T. *Early American Furniture, How to Recognize, Evaluate, Buy, and Care For the Most Beautiful Pieces: High Styles, Country, Primitive, and Rustic.* New York:

Alfred A. Knopf, 1970.

_____. *The Impecunious Collector's Guide to American Antiques.* New York: Alfred A. Knopf, 1975.

_____. *American Furniture and the British Tradition to 1830.* New York: Alfred A. Knopf, 1982.

Lockwood, Luke Vincent. *Colonial Furniture in America.* 2 vols. New York: Charles Scribner's Sons, 1901, 1913. Reprint. New York: Castle Books, 1951.

Lyon, Irving Whitall. *The Colonial Furniture of New England.* Boston: Houghton Mifflin Company, 1891. Reprint. New York: E.P. Dutton, 1977.

Macquoid, Percy. *A History of English Furniture.* 4 vols. London: Collins, 1919. Reprint. New York: Dover Publications, 1972.

Maryland Historical Society. *Furniture in Maryland, 1740-1940.* Baltimore: Maryland Historical Society, 1984.

Miller, Edgar G. *American Antique Furniture, A Book for Amateurs.* 2 vols. 1937. Reprint. New York: Dover Publications, 1966.

Montgomery, Charles F. *American Furniture, The Federal Period ne Henry Francis du Pont Winterthur Museum.* New York: The Viking Press, 1966.

Nutting, Wallace. *Furniture Treasury.* 3 vols. New York: The MacMillan Publishing Company, 1928.

_____. *Furniture of the Pilgrim Century.* 2 vols. 1924. Reprint. New York: Dover Publications, 1965.

Sack, Albert. *Fine Points of Furniture: Early American.* New York: Crown Publishing, 1950.

Schiffer, Nancy N. and Herbert F. *Woods We Live With.* West Chester, Pennsylvania: Schiffer Publishing Ltd., 1977.

Shea, John G. *Antique Country Furniture of North America.* New York: Van Nostrand Reinbold Co., 1975.